The Standard Publishing Company, Cincinnati, Ohio
A division of Standex International Corporation
© 1993 by The Standard Publishing Company
All rights reserved.
Printed in the United States of America
00 99 98 97 96 95 94 93   5 4 3 2 1

Library of Congress Catalog Card Number 92-32818
ISBN 0-7847-0037-0
Cataloging-in-Publication data available

John 21:1-14 retold by
Mark A. Taylor

Breakfast
With
Jesus

illustrated by Andy Stiles

LITTLE DEER
B·O·O·K·S
PSALM 42:1

Standard Publishing
Cincinnati, Ohio

"I'm cold," said Thomas, as the night breeze blew
    across his wet arms.

"Me, too," said Nathanael, and he shivered
    in the creaky boat.

"I'm hungry," said James, as he watched the water and their empty fishing net.

"Me, too," said John, and his stomach growled and rumbled.

All the fishermen laughed—

—all except Peter.
"Keep fishing!" he commanded. "It's almost morning,
and we haven't caught a thing." Peter sighed. "I
wish Jesus were here," he said to himself. "I hope
we'll see him again soon."
Just then the fishermen heard a voice from far away.

"FRIENDS!"

said the voice.
"Who's that?"
asked Thomas.

"Do you have any fish?"

"It's coming from the shore!" said John.

The fishermen didn't know what to think. They didn't know what to say. They peered through the fog and saw a man on the land.

"Do you have

any fish?"
the man called again.

"**No,**" said Thomas and Nathanael, James and John.
"**No,**" said Peter.
"**No!**" said all the cold and hungry fishermen in the creaky boat on the quiet lake.

And then the man said something quite surprising . . .

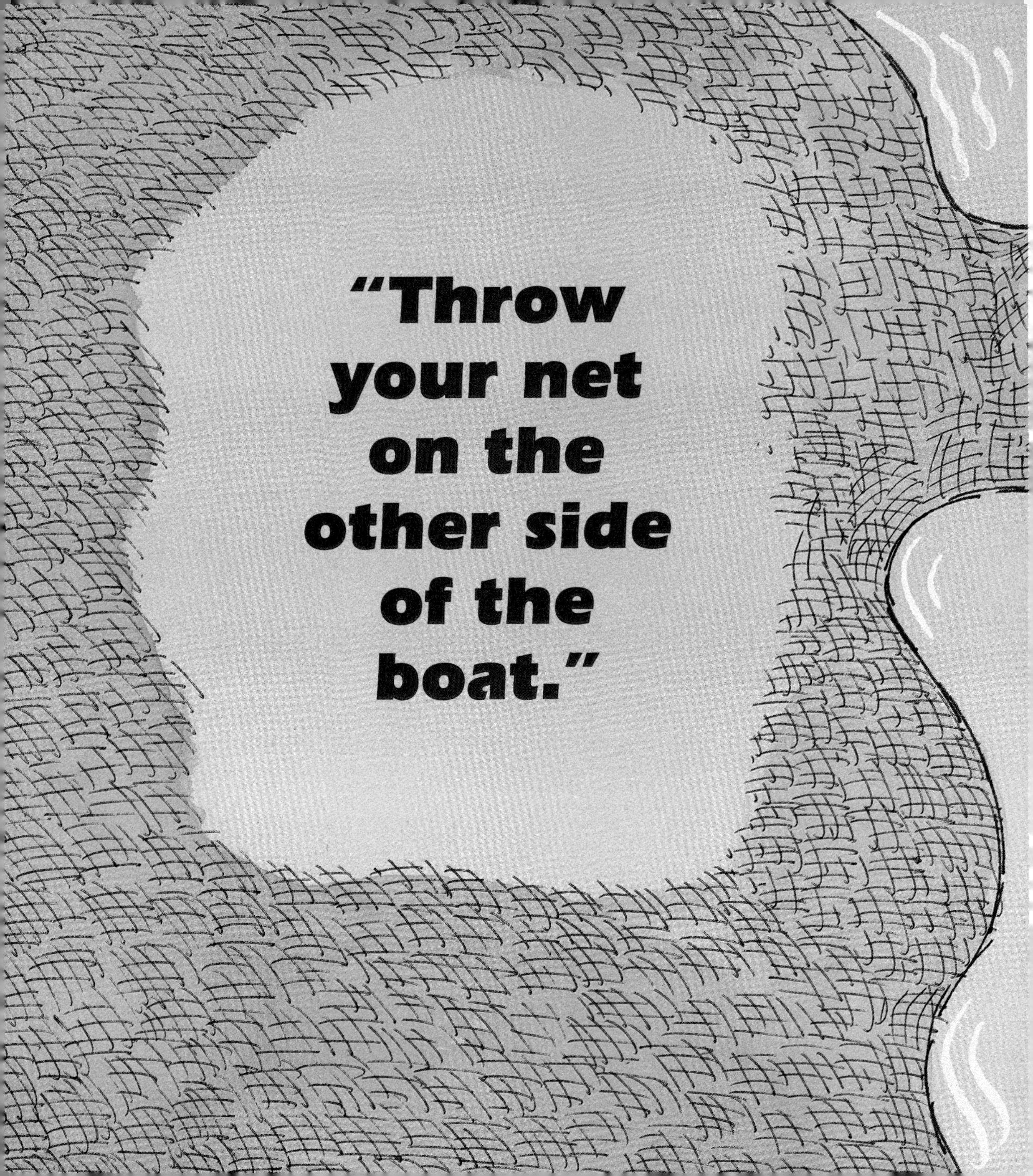

"Throw your net on the other side of the boat."

Thomas looked at Nathanael.
James looked at John.
They all looked at Peter.
And Peter said,
"OK, let's try it."

The fishermen tugged the heavy net out of the water
and into the boat. Not one fish was in the net.
Then they heaved the net back into the water on
the other side of the boat.

"There," said Thomas. "We did what he said. But what difference does it make? We'll never catch any fish tonight."

And then it happened!

FISH!

The net was full of fish!

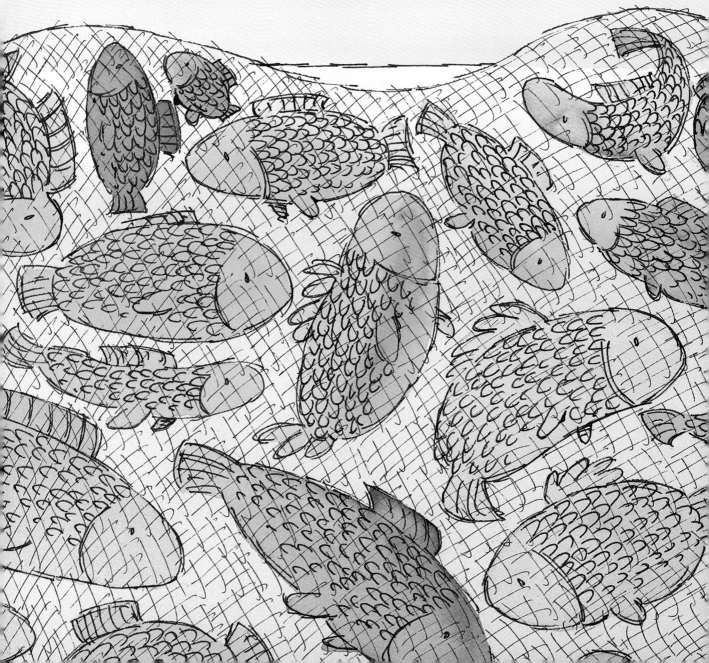

swimming,

flipping,

flopping fish!

The net bulged
and almost broke.
The men could not
haul it back into
the boat.

John stared across the water at the man still watching from the shore. "It's Jesus," he said. "It's Jesus! Jesus is the one who told us where to fish!"

"I want to see him!" said Peter.
Peter dove into the lake.

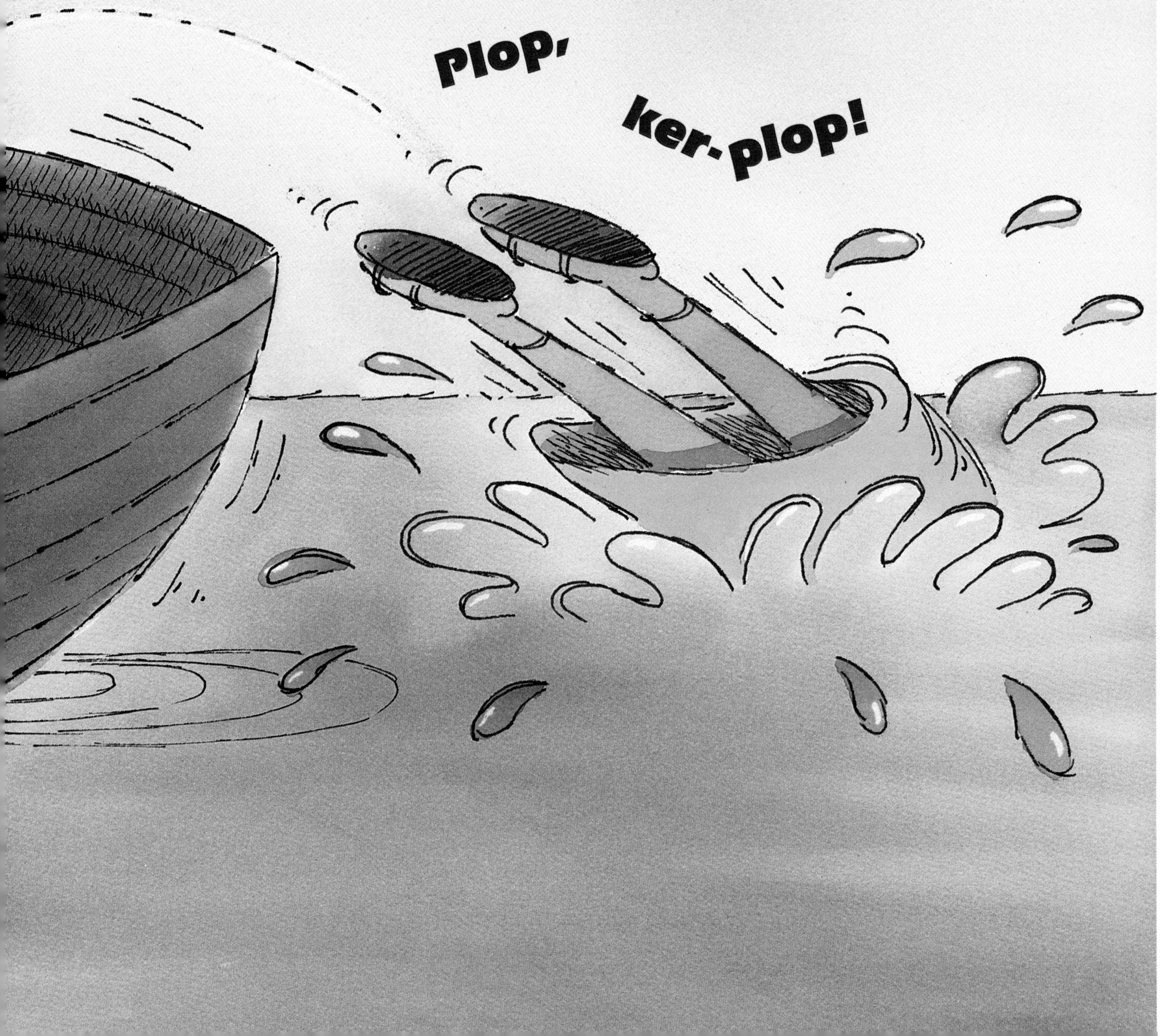

"Jesus told us he would meet us!"
he remembered as he swam.
Left arm, right arm!
"Jesus told us he would live forever!"
Kick hard! Hurry, hurry!
"Jesus died once, but never again!"

Peter smiled as he sloshed out of the water onto the sandy shore. There was Jesus, cooking fish over a small fire of hot coals.

Pop!

Sizzle!

Pop!

Soon the other fishermen brought the boat to land, dragging their net full of fish. "Come and have breakfast with me," Jesus said.

Jesus gave them bread and fish to eat. "Thank you, God, for our food," he said.

"Thank you for my fishermen friends. Thank you for letting me live again, even after I was dead."

Now Thomas and Nathanael were warm, sitting by the
fire Jesus made. And James and John were full,
eating the tasty breakfast Jesus cooked.

And Peter—well, Peter sat on the seashore and munched his breakfast and talked with Jesus all morning long.

He couldn't have been happier!